Palimpsest of Ghosts

Collected Poems

Macaque

By the same author:

Poetry

A Man Remembers (2016)

As one of the Writers in Stone

Driftwood (2019)
Cuckoo (2021)

Writing as Hamish MacNeil

The Strange Discoveries at Wimblestone Road (2021)

Second Edition 2021

ISBN 978-1-8384346-3-2

©2017 Macaque

For my parents, and for
Harry, Cameron, Ellis and Charlie

Acknowledgements

I am deeply indebted to a great many people for their support and encouragement over the years. This volume would not have been possible without the help of the following: my parents, Anthony Grantham, The Victoria Park Poetry Group and The Benjamin Society, Lutterworth Writers Group, Weston Poets, Melanie Branton and Jim Barron, Writers in Stone, The Lymers, Louise Hill and Rebecca Tantonay, and all at Wordmustard and Café Sketch where many of these poems first aired.

CONTENTS

Faith	7
Dunnottar	8
Chopin	9
Diane	10
Haiku of Self	11
Autumn	12
50 Words About Love	13
Three Poems	14
Time and Time Again	16
The Pigeon	17
Haiku by Candlelight	18
Shadows	19
Fingers	20
Abacus	21
Reflective Sestina	22
Prose Poem: Snow	24
A Classical Lament	26
Haunted	27
Daughter	28
Sans Titre	29
La Flamme	30
St Etienne	31
Clown	32

From *A Man Remembers*

Flatmate	35
Angelika	36
Reading Between the Lashes	37
History	38
My Father	40
Myosotis	41
The Ash Garden	42
In the Grass	43

February	44
The Window	45
How Do I Tell You?	46
The Art of Cruelty	48
Bump in the Night	49
Harbinger	50
After Pushkin	52
Mahogany	53
Beach	54
Evensong	55
Trompe L'Oreille	59
Untitled	60
The Flame	61
St Etienne	62
Hidden Tracks	63

Faith

She rises and shimmies
To the window, shaking the night
From her hair. Outside

In the gloom, the used car lot
Slumbers on, a slow train lumbers
Its clanking bulk like a grotesque
Worm, scraps of damp litter lag
The railings. Beyond her

Silhouette, the grey clouds blush,
Pinking with light from the cracked
Eye of the horizon. She stretches

Feline, goes on tiptoes, leans
Her weight on the heels of her palms, tips
Forward, tilts her head, presses, squashes, crams
Her face into the corner of the window frame,
Cheek against the cold glass,
Looking.

I love watching this ritual.
Her bare legs dangling like elegant pendula
Beneath the hem of her nightshirt.

Fixing her face like this, looking far
Far to the left, under the eaves of the terrace,
Through the trees that border the road in its
Ascension, she can almost see the place
Where the cathedral is.

And I know that she is smiling.

Dunnottar

Black eye and white
Wings over white
Water on black rock

White wing on the blue wind
A black call in the steep drop

The stone's fall and the wave's roll
Stalk bend, leaf loll
The sun's beat, cliff's heat
Blonde curls over bare feet

Pale lips over white teeth
Black heart and the heart's beat

The heart's beat

Chopin

Chopin had the sensitive feet
The very air seemed brittle about him

He walked barefoot over the parquet floor
A long polished gallery sweet to the eye
In morning's lucid tears

He picked his way lightly across the keyboard
Pattern of sunlit panes and shadow frames
As the trapped air cut and sliced his soles
Piercing the soft skin like the gem shards
Of Champagne glasses

The room shone with tranquil incomprehension
This lithe figure so serene, squeezing
Aural ecstasy from the pure globes of blood
Under his feet

I tried it, naked at dawn, walking over
Glass-dusted polished boards in sunlight sandals
The wood groaning as I ground in the slivers
And I in my own pair of fairy glass slippers
But nothing more

I bled and got glass in my feet, blood on the floor
And a sense of failure. My blood contains no notes
My feet are not sensitive
My floor is ruined

Chopin had the sensitive feet
His blood was brittle with staccato genius

Diane

She
With quill fingers raking sand
Flutters toes in flocks of foam
        Her
Spoon smile spilling lava laughter
                She
Catches stone blue with one hand

                        She
With coral tongue tearing silence
Etches dreams among the grains
                Her
Cobalt eyes closed tickle-feet tight
        She
Spills her smile of viscous joy
Again

Haiku of Self

Each day, the mirror
Shows me a different face
But always my own.

Each day an older
Face bearing different scars,
A different pain,

Thicker stubble to
Shave again, another grey
Hair, a deeper frown.

But over each I
Still perceive my earlier
Semblances of self.

Is this what the world
Sees, this parade of masks,
This palimpsest of ghosts?

Autumn

Post coital season,
Filling the silence
After summer's sighs,
Cooling like lust, dimming
Into dream colour.

Trees release their leaves
Like an orgasm,
Stark and vulnerable,
Their bare cadence echoing
Your limbs. Presently,

These grey sheets in the dawn
Light will be cold as snow,
Empty as the boughs but
For the faint scent of jasmine.

And all I can do is wait.

50 Words About Love

All that pain
You caused, and she
Loved you; the loss of
Sleep, the worry,
Your frequent indifference,
All the times
You never listened, and still
She loved you.

And you met others
Who loved you
For a while, a lesser
Love, an imitation.

Then this;
And now you know.

Three Poems

I. Sunday Haiku

Working late, my thoughts
Stray to Lisa's caramel
Skin in the moonlight

To every curve, swell
Crease and dimple, envious
Even of the breeze

That knows the delight
Of her touch, her scent, her taste,
Knows, but will not tell.

II. Thoughts of Lisa (Sleeping)

My caramel kitten
My little madness
My smouldering ecstasy
My antidote to sadness

Sleeping soundly
You cannot see
How completely
You undo me

III. Caramel Sunrise

I open my eyes
To your face rising from a
Sea of pale pillow

Nose the horizon
The golden dome of your cheek
Glowing like the sun

Your unblinking eye
Watches me with feline gaze
As I hold you in my palm
Just a photograph

Time and Time Again

It takes the patience born
Of solitude to see it,
To watch the tide return
Time and time again;

To watch the waves rush
Like prodigals
At the waiting rocks;
To watch the white blood
Fly at the pounding,
The salt scars borne away
Time and time again;

To witness the impassive bearing
Of the rocks, the relentless
Folly of the tide,
And to realise.

You were my rock,
The one I rushed the flat expanse for
When the work-tide brought me back.
You let me break
My heart against you
Time and time again.

The Pigeon

In the spring our fledgling
Love cried wide-mouthed with
Hunger. We fed it every hour,
Juicy worm to eager beak, sneaking
Into its tight nest for comfort.

Sudden summer swooped the blue
Sky, a whoop and a cry, and our
Love rose to the call of its kind,
Our nest left empty, our egg-shell
Hearts cold.

                Just yesterday
I passed a broken pigeon on the
Verge, chest skyward, heart wild
With pain, little pink legs twitching
Stupidly, one rigid, broken wing
Pointing me onward.

Haiku By Candlelight

Patient flame, tethered
To the moist wick; elegance
In captivity.

In your yearning form
I learn to balance myself,
Calm my own flicker

Reach without jumping,
Sway without falling, nourish
The bright heart of me.

In you I find my
Own wick-root to strain against
To light up the world.

Shadows

Soft as shadows on silk
The ghost of your breath
In the moonlight. Your cooling skin

Losing lustre, sinks in
To my flesh. I feel the weight
Of you return, the pulse
Of you steady, I feel the minutes
Well and spill

Like tears, watching you sleep
Watching the sky shimmer, watching
The wind chase shadows over silk

Fingers

How I envy your fingers!
I watch them
As they play with your hair
And I begin to think of
Their other inevitable journeys.

How I envy your fingers!
They are always
So close to you and so expressive.
They tell me what you are feeling
And I wish they were mine.

How I envy your fingers!
I imagine them
Gently arousing you,
Pressing against your beautiful frame,
Clawing at some man's back
How I hate your cruel fingers!

But still, how I envy them.
I melt as
They tease your lips in conversation,
But most of all I desire to be
The one you suck covered in cream.

Abacus

A year ago I held you,
Weighing you against the bulk
Of my loneliness, measuring

The length of you against
The emptiness inside me,
Marvelling at the fit of you

In my palms, against my hips,
My lips, your ear in the scallop of my
Collar bone, unaware

That I was counting on
The abacus of your ribs
The hours until you left.

Reflective Sestina

Pale, sleeping open-mouthed
In an old chair bolstered with
Pillows, my mother's mother
Spends her last days
Quietly snoring. Her dreams
Are not for me to remember.

But there is much I do remember
Of being young and sticky-mouthed
In need of comfort from bad dreams.
Then, she would distract me with
Stories from her younger days,
Tales I never heard from my mother.

Such fading histories of her own mother
Are the things I feel I should remember
In this new awareness of the limit of our days,
To sit in my dotage by the grate fiery-mouthed
Enthralling some future generation with
Fables capable of stirring their dreams.

But for now it is my gran who dreams,
Providing respite for my harried mother,
And taunting my guilty conscience with
Thoughts that this will be better to remember
Than the pain-induced foul-mouthed
Episodes that frequently punctuate her days.

So I try to focus on my childhood days,
On images hard to distinguish from dreams,
When the summer mornings were candy-mouthed,
And afternoons spent with my grandmother

Playing hands of cards. I still remember
The Gas Board promotional pack we played with.

Connecting these memories now, with
The frail old woman counting her days,
I wonder if she, too, is prone to remember,
If these are the images recurring in her dreams,
Or does she dwell on the death of her mother,
Or wartime friends who died broken-mouthed?

And will she remember the times I mouthed,
With a wave, 'I love you' from the arms of my mother?
Must each of our days return in tomorrow's dreams?

Prose Poem: Snow

You are out walking. You are alone.
You are wearing your blue jeans, with the leather
Belt she bought you years ago, a white T-shirt
And a thick, blue sweater. You have your coat fastened;
Your hands are in your pockets. You are walking quickly,
Your head down. You can see your booted feet striding
Rhythmically. You watch them, hypnotized, unaware
Of your surroundings.

You can feel the cold air on your cheeks
Like the rasp of a cat's tongue. You sense
The imminent arrival of snow: the air
Feels taut like a harp string, like a
Drum skin.

You straighten, slowing down. You look
Up at the heavy sky.
You stop.
You can see the wisps of your breath as
They unfurl against the darker grey of the clouds.
You wait.

There is music in the falling of snow.
You listen, now, waiting. Your breath stills;
Your feet become cold. You start to feel
Dizzy staring at the visual equivalent of silence.
You can feel the earth's rotation, you sense
The slow beating of its heart. You stand and
Wait in the cold, your head back, your
Fists clenched in your pockets.

And now you hear the plucking of the harp,

The brushing of the drum. You hear
The flakes' glissando, hear them ring
In their fall, struck by air, by thoughts, by cold
Expectant glances. And out of the grey sky
You see them, like coins dropped into a pool,
You see them sinking through the cold air
Towards you.

There is a pattern to the falling of snow. You
Watch, now, smiling. Staring at the vast
Palimpsest of sky, you note the rhythms,
The dances, trace the tumbles and swirls,
The repetitions, see how one flake takes up
Where another gave out, piece together the
Harmony, the coded choreography. You watch,
Still smiling, still standing. The cold has become
Part of you. You are like a stargazer mapping
Ever changing constellations, watching the history
Of the universe unfold in one evening, watching
For the face of a lost love, listening for her voice
In the chorus of falling ice.

You take your hands out of your pockets
And raise your arms, cruciform, feeling the
Rhythm tapped out on your palms, listening
To the voice that speaks with a soft, wet tongue,
That sings and dances with more meaning than
You can contain. You are smiling. And you
Are crying. Standing in the open with your arms
Raised, blurring with the white that falls all around you.
Your fingers are red, your face is pale, your feet
Are hidden beneath a gauze of flakes. You are singing.
There is music in the falling of snow.
There is madness in the listening.

A Classical Lament

"The greatest crime of this age, I find,
Is developing a healthy body
Ahead of a fertile mind.
And thus it is, young sirs,
That I shall be glad when I am blind."

The Latin master paused
To lip his pipe, and then opined
Of the one who rivalled Homer's Helen,
Especially from behind:

"Faced with conjugation,
She declined."

Haunted

In the embraces of princesses
And the company of whores
I have thought and talked
And dreamed of you
Transposing their caresses
And vulgar chores
Through memory
Wishing all their fragrant tresses
Each sigh, each kiss
Each proffered orifice
Were yours

Daughter

And the future
Stretches on without
Her. I bear the

Absence, kernel of my
Heart, like an embryo,
A weight of unvoiced love.

She was sweet as nectar,
Her mother's daughter,
An image of innocence and

Hellenic beauty, immeasurable;
Absolute. And now the future
Stretches on without

Her knowing that
All my thoughts flail after
Her, day after day.

Sans Titre

La fumée commence
A côté du verre,
En face de la bouteille,
Une cigarette abondonée sur le cendrier.

Elle vit, elle court,
Verticale d'abord,
Puis elle se donne
Aux courants de la petite atmosphère.

Elle saute, spirale,
Toujours si pâle,
Elle sursaut en haut
De la bouteille
Et le verre
Et la table,
Avant de se dissiper en l'air.

Et la chaise
Poussée de la table,
Et l'homme par terre?

Nous sommes tous
Les cigarettes,
Nous sommes tous
La fumée,
Nous sommes tout

Allume moi.

Translation on page 60

La Flamme

La flamme, la flamme,
Chuchotant tendres secrets
La flamme, la flamme,
Eteignant l'obscurité
La flamme, la flamme,
Brûlant sans regrets
La flamme, la flamme,
Dont toute nature est née
La flamme, la flamme,
Mon âme la flame,
Nos vies vacillent ensemble,
Nos vies vacillent dans l'ombre.

Translation on page 61

St Etienne
La Ville en Hiver

Elle dort
Au pied des collines
Comme un chaton sur une couette;
Une coquette neuve et blanche
Comme la neige qui la câline,
Cachant les feuilles mortes des arbres,
Cachant les larmes gelées
Jusqu'au printemps.
Elle ronronne tranquillement avec le son
Des trams, et ses yeux demi-fermés
Pétillent dans l'obscurité.

Elle dort, mais elle rêve,
Comme un pays qui est en grève.

Translation on page 62

Clown

The circus is illusory. Only
The clown's tears are real. The acrobats

Are geometers tumbling in arcs of
Clear number, all trajectories ratified and proven;

The wire walkers toe the line:
High above the safety net

To upturned gaze the cable looks
Cobweb-thin. The drummer's snare

Promises the danger, the audience
Gets caught up within. But

The clown under his painted smile
Fills his comic shoe with foot, feels

Every honk of soft, red nose. Cast out,
Misunderstood, a quiet child not like

The rest, flushing pheasants in the woods,
Watching hatchlings in their nests,

He never does what he expects.

From "A Man Remembers"

A Man Remembers was published in 2016 as a limited edition of signed and hand numbered copies. The collection was united by the theme of memories and featured Janka Bresznicka's In The Grass on the cover.

Flatmate

Newly bathed, damp and fragrant,
She entered loosely wrapped
In towel and robe. Calm,
Refreshed, she smiled,
Looked sweet. Bending
Before the fire, drying
Hair that clung impishly
About her face, the robe
Fell gently open to reveal

To reveal the substance
Of thought and dream:
Her skin, her breast, her nipple.

I imagine.
I turned away.

Angelika

She is beautiful,
Vivid as bright blossom on dark boughs
Budding in spring sunlight, when the warm
Breeze is full of promise as it soughs
And the air is full of birdsong from the dawn.

She is beautiful,
Fresh like summer mornings after nights of rain
When cheek soft petals drip with scent, and all is still
But for a tardy fox or badger down the lane,
And nothing ever seemed more perfect, nor ever will.

She is beautiful,
Sweet as autumn mist laced with leafy smoke
When the trees in all their mineral hues stand proud,
And the earth is splendid in its golden cloak,
And the setting sun makes candyfloss of the cloud.

She is beautiful,
With brumal eyes like jewels in a mountain lake
And lips like berries on a frosted bush.
Her face is the one I would see when I awake,
Her smile the one I want my lips to brush.
She is beautiful.

Reading Between the Lashes

Hard to gauge the impact
On a child of five,
Finding the carcass of a lamb
Born eyeless,
The backs of busy flies
Shining in the dark sockets;
But I never could bear eye contact.

I never could read between the lines,
Could never see the pain contradict your lips,
Listened only to the language
Of your lips uncontradicted.
I never registered the mute cries
Hidden by my averted eyes.

I was much older the day you turned
Your tame canals into rivers of meaning.

History

This plague of warm nights, mercurial
Shimmers on the high tide, leaning late
On the sea wall, watching the amblers,
Listening to the waves and the
Gifts of the breeze

I think of Lotte
Bathing naked that summer,
Wet hair in the wind, winding up
The narrow streets
Like a bee
On her yellow Vespa.

We picked sackfuls of blueberries
In the forest with her Grandpapa,
Losing ourselves in the trees, stealing
Glances, touches, kisses
While the old man rambled.

Then sprinkling sugar over hot
Blueberry pie, and hands of cards
At her Grandma's solid table,
Her blue summer dress, bare arms,
Bare legs, slipping a foot
From a sandal.

And later, opening the shutters
To the moon and the scent of
Pipe tobacco,
Watching her breasts as she slept
In the pallid light and
Attic heat.

History, you bastard,
Repeat! Repeat! Repeat!

My father

My father found a new leg
Buried in a block of wood.
He saw it before I did, peeling back
The curls with curved blades to show me,
Then wiping it bone clean with rough paper.

We painted it together, applied the varnish,
Until it matched the rocking horse I had broken.

I held those blades years later,
All arranged in a tan leather pouch,
Rusted slightly, the smooth handles
Darkened by his grip.
I zipped them up slowly,
The tools that couldn't fix him.

Myosotis

I will always remember that kiss
And the taste of your smile
And the way that we talked
Without words for a while
And the feeling of absolute bliss
I will always remember that kiss

I will always remember that day
And the look in your eyes
And the feel of your skin and your hair
And the sound of your sighs
And the warmth of the sun
On the couch where we lay
I will never forget

I will always remember the joy of that kiss
And try not to compare it to this
And my feelings of sorrow, despair and regret
That I cannot return to a time that I miss

The Ash Garden

The Garden was untamed, sprawling,
A natural joy. I came alive there,
Walking with the half-blind Bones
Through the trees, by the glint
And gurgle of the stream,
In the company of Wild Garlic.

Pale Ash would settle, deep,
Soft like summer snow. I loved
The sound it made,
Harmony in the branches,
Laughter in the leaves,
Pervasive beauty.

Even now, I find smudges of grey
On my clothes, and green fronds
And blades of grass,
And wonder how long
My footprints will last.

In the Grass
(Janka Bresznicka, Acrylic, 2010)

Through long tresses
Of dry blond grasses
The wind insinuates a face.

Tips tickle the rippled surface
Of the sky, birds beat
Dark wings on blue heat.

Eyes and fingers meet among
The flattened stems, touches long
Awaited brave the silent afternoon.

Time distils to one drop, drunk too soon.
Lying together as the day grows shorter,
The poet and the artist's daughter.

February

I stop and listen in the stillness,
In the held breath of silence
Before the snow falls, listen

For your voice, the gentle assault
Of your laughter, strain all my
Feral senses to snare a hint of you.

The flakes fall with tenderness,
Landing lip-soft on long stones,
Pooling on the grass like wet light,

Cold as unworn silk, bending boughs
With the weight to break hearts
Not branches. They brush my skin

Like kitten paws, pad upon hood
And shoulders, settle, bind, conquer,
Cover a stone angel's frozen tears.

Drifts swell with your soft cheek's curve,
Twigs arch like dark brows, glancing berries
Glisten with cruel frost. The churchyard

Buries its head while I cannot; beauty
Still holds the eye, though love is lost.

The Window

Afterwards, my old sweater
Cupping your arse, you leaned
Into the moonlight and fox
Calls for recovery, while

I lay in that hollow
Of subsided exertion, watching
The worked wool pull
Taut, watching the smoke
Fray, watching you,
An ocular orgasm. I rose

To join you, hold you,
Reclaim you, envious
Of your cigarette.

How Do I Tell You?

The night was warm,
Alive with the craze
Of crickets and the sea's devotions
To the sandy shore,

And the girl brought me a mango.
At seventeen, I had never tasted the fruit.

She split it deftly in the dark,
Slicing each half with the knife
She wore at her hip, watched me
Like a cat as I took my first bite,
The juice sweet,
Texture like honeyed flesh.

We ate in silence,
The juice coating our chins,
Netting us with the sweet aroma,
The scent of complicity,

And when we kissed,
She tasted of Heaven, of mango
And desire and life, of the sea
And the beach and the breeze,
My whole world shrunk to the tip
Of her deliciously sticky tongue.

Last night
You opened a tin of sliced mango,
Serving the cold juicy tongues
Into two bowls with the spoon
You keep in the pot by the hob.

We ate in silence
As the taste and texture transported
Me to a warm, dark beach
By a fragrant grove,
And when we kissed,
You tasted of disappointment.

The Art of Cruelty
(On seeing two paintings by Ian Brady
Reproduced in a newspaper)

Who is the sad Christ
Whose African head rises
A tracheal tornado of
Devil red dust?
What games of lust
Won and lost in the shadows of
That satanic mill piece crown?

And you, with the patience to paint wallpaper,
And the time now to paint wallpaper,
And the wall beneath the peeling paper,
And a beetle on the wall beneath the paper
Will earn no sympathy,
No respect with this self-conscious desolation.

Listen:
The wolf-world still bays for your blood.
Your broken pawns in the unmarked earth
Will not be forgotten.

Bump in the Night

We feel you ticking
In the darkness, our
Fat gold watch wound with love,

Ticking strong, eager kicks,
Hands tracing the surface,
Marking time until we see you.

We wait patiently, your
Hope-coiled spring
Fascinates, the quiet chiming

Of your hours already
Dictates our sleep.
We wait to meet you

When you are you,
And no longer
The bump in the night.

Harbinger

August night,
Moon-shadows, susurrus,
And the cerebral nudge of fox.

I sense
Before I see it
Nose out of the leaf-dark,
Crossing the quiet street
Like a rusted memory, fur
The colour of dried blood.

Ephemeral, it nimble-slips
Between the bins, a bobbin
Pulling a frayed thread,
Red on silver and gone
Red on silver
Gone

Tugging the night behind it
Through the shadows

Red. Black.
Gone.

Tugging at the memory,
Unspooling my mind
Red on silver
And gone.

I watch it weave from
Garden to garden, through
Fence and gate and bush,

Fox-bobbin, red on silver
Red on black
And gone

The moon aches in the
Cloud slicked sky,
Now as before, when I
Sensed,
And woke for no reason
To see the pattern you had left
On the weft of life

Red on silver
And gone
Like a fox frisking the moonlight
With russet paws.

Then as now, the tears
Were mine, but the blood
Was yours.

After Pushkin

Not in Russia, Pushkin,
No, not here,
But I, too, have seen them,
These galvanising girls,
And shared your lascivious thoughts,
Pushkin.

Not in the drear Russian winter,
No, not here,
But I have followed them
From terraces and tall, arched windows,
From leaned-upon white balustrades
And floated-down wide stone steps,
My thoughts have followed them
Into the night so cricket-thick
With the throb of sex,
The rousing rubbing of legs on legs
In breathless rhythm.

Their bare breasts
Made me smile, too,
Pushkin.

Mahogany

This hotel is near the station,
In a back street. The trains breathe
Hard against the windows, rattling
The dark panes, the wine bottles,
Nerves like ice in a tumbler.

The cardboard mats are worn
And ringed, the wood dull under
Flaky varnish, the bruised brass
Belongs to this dimness.

Always the little details.

Another train, and the room shudders
Like a last orgasm before sleep.
I am doomed to wonder
How the polished mahogany shone;
How the optics rattled against
The bar they raped you on.

Beach

At the cliff's foot
Rocks concede to sand
With wild elegance and
Rugged grace. Gulls cut

And plunge the heights,
Courting winds that burn
The face with stern
Bluffs of salt and spice.

Waves rush, curl like tongues
To kiss stones that rasp
In the cold wake, gasp
And chuckle in unison
With my enraptured sons.

Evensong

Light fades. Light and life,
Colour, beauty, happiness all
Fade.

Age is the only contrary thing,
For even pain fades
With time, memories all fade,
And pain is a kind of memory.

We are all born
In winter, and die
In winter, symbol
Of our senses' austerity:

Life is bare and cold
For the very young
And very old.

But I am not so old,
Not yet. I still have seasons
To endure; memories to make
And to forget, more beauty
And colour to watch fade, and to lament.

What am I?

Regard me here as
I lounge and loaf,
Lounge and loaf at my leisure,
Watching a slender piece of ass.

A summer spear of a girl goes

By, oblivious.
All go by,
Though some linger like scent
In an empty room
Until breathing becomes unbearable.
All things become unbearable.

What am I? What
Have I become?

I am the ruin
Of the round hands' tumble,
Chaff of the great globe's
Scything circle.
I am a straw man,
A hollow man twisting
In the wind
Like a talisman,
Like an offering to the gods.
A wicker man
Spreading my ashen flesh
Over earth's bone.

In the quiet hours, a man
Remembers.

Come,
Sit with me
Under the eye-wide lens of sky,
Here, where the light still lingers,
The changing light that changes
Everything with it, structure,
Hue and distance all
Dependent upon the light.

Listen:
Hear the stumbling ring
Of the swung bells falling
Onto their hammers in the
Stone tower, calling the faithful.

Out here, belief is easier,
Here, where the shadows stir
At the edges of the thin air
Objects blur into spaces,
We feel the connection

Senses attune to the unseen.

Beyond loam and lichen,
Squirrel, beetle, stamen,
We feel the earth's pulse,
Feel the power and purpose
Of the wind.

Sit with me,
Sit.
Watch the path of the wind
That turns the leaves and grasses
Pale and black,
The sudden wind that tightens
The skin, pulls us closer.

Remind yourself:
This is what we have forgotten.

The church of small stones alters nothing
But the low horizon, the earth beats
With its own rhythm, and in

The quiet hours, a man remembers,
All the faded things return.

All the faded things return.

Trompe L'Oreille
(For Mari)

St Margaret's East with West
Wellow, after the rain.

Cresting a slight rise,
At the end of a quiet, narrow lane,
Dark coastal stones glisten like eyes
As the black cloud gathers again,
And follows you in.

We each have our reasons
And our ways;
Our guided recollections
And quiet introspections,
Encompassing the seasons
And recent days.

But the memory I will
Never shake, coupled with the image
Of a tree and fresh earth on a green hill:

Your sister
Reading your words
With your voice.

Translations

Untitled

The smoke starts
Next to the glass
Opposite the bottle
A cigarette abandoned in the ashtray

It lives, it courses
Vertical at first
Then gives itself
To the currents of the little room

It jumps, spirals,
Always so pale,
It summersaults above
The bottle
And the glass
And the table
Before dissipating into the air

And the chair,
Pushed from the table,
And the man on the floor?

We are all smoke
We are all cigarettes
We are everything

Light me

The Flame

The flame, the flame,
Whispering tender secrets
The flame, the flame,
Extinguishing the darkness
The flame, the flame,
Burning without regret
The flame, the flame,
From which all nature is born
The flame, the flame,
My soul the flame,
Our lives flicker together,
Our lives flicker in the darkness.

St Etienne
The Town in Winter

She sleeps
At the foot of the hills
Like a kitten on a duvet;
A duvet new and white
Like the snow that hugs her,
Hiding the russet of the trees
Hiding the frozen tears
Until spring.
She snores gently with the sound
Of trams, and her half closed eyes
Sparkle in the darkness.

She sleeps, but dreams,
Like a country on strike.

Hidden Tracks – Micro Poems

Black cat
Curious claws
Such a handsome hindrance

***

Revolution

Beneath the deep
And even snow
Green grass is growing

***

Incandescent moon
Pale as a raw, peeled onion
Brings tears to my eyes

***

Outside the stable
Of the dying horse
Black cat is

***

Soft earth
How quickly we forget
Our childhood

***

Moist lips
Red cheeks
The steam from her coffee

***

Writing cock in hand
Students will one day lap up
My ejaculate

***

Gnarled oaks in the park
Barking your twisted faces
Leaving in the spring

***

A zest of moon rind
Milk white, like a memory
Seasoning the sky

***

Canvas of blue shapes
Eyes listening to a language
That they do not speak

***

Rough stone, weathered wood
An old barn becomes a home –
The difference love makes

ABOUT THE AUTHOR

Macaque lives in rural Somerset in a village surrounded by cider orchards. He is a keen photographer, an enthusiastic guitar player, and a lover of unspoilt nature, especially hills, coastlines and lakeshores.

Writing as Hamish MacNeil, he has recently published his first novel *The Strange Discoveries at Wimblestone Road*, a children's fantasy story set in the Mendip hills. He has more novels percolating, and hopes to publish a second volume of poetry, *Mosaic*, in 2021.

Printed in Great Britain
by Amazon

65798287R00038